THE BOOK OF JEWISH JOYS (NO OYS).

DOODLE PAW PRESS

DEDICATED

To my family.

By Amanda Minuk

Designed in Canva. All images licensed from Canva.com
Cover- Challah,Pixelshot; Purim,tomertu, Getty Images; Apples,smirart, Getty Images ; Shofar, tovfla, Getty Images Signature; Hamentashen, tovfla, Getty Images Signature; Chanukah, valentynsemenov , Shabbat, BigNazik, Getty Images; Bagels , Creatas Images, Photo images

Page 1- jewish star, Jenny Lipets
Page 3- Challah,Pixelshot; Purim,tomertu, Getty Images; Apples,smirart, Getty Images ; Shofar, tovfla, Getty Images Signature; Hamentashen, tovfla, Getty Images Signature; Chanukah, valentynsemenov ,
Page 6 - (stellalevi, Getty Images Signature)
Page 8- Pixelshot
Page 10- smirart, Getty Images
Page 12- tovfla, Getty Images Signature
Page 14- tovfla, Getty Images Signature
Page 16- Maya Holt, corelens
Page 18- mtreasure, Getty Images Signature
Page 20 - fotofrog, Getty Images Signature
Page 22- Creatas Images, Photo images
Page 24-
Top- Jupiterimages, Photo Images
Middle (one from Getty Images)
Bottom- Billion Photos
Page 26- A_Lein, Getty Images
Page 28- Nataly Hanin, Getty Images
Page 30- CatLane, Getty Images Signature
Page 32- Geshas, Getty Images
Page 34- Neniya, Getty Images
Page 36- liorpt, Getty Images
Page 38- Billion Photos
Page 40 -SMarina, Getty Images
Page 42- Jess Lessard, Getty Images
Page 44- Mariha-kitchen , Getty Images
Page 46- Nataly Hanin, Getty Images
Page 48- kornyeyeva. Getty Images
Page 50 - alisafarov, Getty Images
Page 54- tovfla, Getty Images Signature
Page 56- Nicole Schlepp, baseimage
Page 58- valentynsemenov
Page 60- tomertu, Getty Images Page Page
Page 62- BigNazik, Getty Images
Page 64- John Theodor, Getty Images
Page 66- tomertu, Getty Images
Page 68- MrButterworth, Getty Images
Page 72- Jason Finn, Getty Images
Page 74- tovfla, Getty Images Signature
Page 78- tovfla, Getty Images Signature
Page 80 - alefbet, Getty Images
Page 88- MikeCherim, Getty Images Signature
Page 94- paulprescott72, Getty Images
Page 96- edu_castro27 pixabay

Copyright © 2022 Doodle Paw Press
ISBN: 978-1-990730-11-5
Hardcover Edition

All rights reserved.
No part of this publication may be reproduced, stored in a retrieval system, or transmitted in any form or by any means, electronic, mechanical, photocopying, recording or otherwise, without written permission of the publisher.

NO OYS ALLOWED
Some kvetching tolerated.

HOW TO READ THIS BOOK

This book shares 72 small, but wonderful things, about being Jewish.

There are a lot of OYs that come with being a Jew, but also a lot of joy. Now more than ever, we need to remember these joys.

This book is a celebration of Jewish culture and pays tribute to the beauty of traditions that date back thousands of years.

The order of the book doesn't matter. You can read it from front to back or back to front or just flip through it here and there.

There are three sections: Jewish Food, Jewish Celebrations and Cultural Fun.

This is not a definitive list, and you may not agree with all the 'joys'- but perhaps that itself is part of the joy- being able to think about and discuss the small and beautiful things about being Jewish.

Remember- no oys allowed.

PART ONE

JEWISH FOOD

1. Slurping your matzah ball soup.

DID YOU KNOW?

Matzah balls are Jewish dumplings. Also known as "knaidel", most often served in chicken soup.

INTERESTING FACT

2. The sweet smell of freshly baked challah.

DID YOU KNOW?

Braiding the Shabbat challah bread began in the late 1400s.

On Rosh Hashana we eat round challahs which represents the circular nature of life and seasons.

3. Expertly dipping your apples in honey- without it dripping on your fingers- to celebrate a sweet new year.

DID YOU KNOW?

The custom of apples and honey started in Ashkenazi Jewish communities in medieval Europe. The first written mention at Rosh Hashanah was in the year 1100.

4. A gooey bite of hamentashen on Purim.

DID YOU KNOW?

Hamentashen are in the shape of a triangle with a yummy filling, such as poppy seed.

The triangle shape represents Haman's hat.

5. The sizzle latkes make on the frying pan.

DID YOU KNOW?

We eat fried foods during Hanukkah to remember the miracle of a small amount of oil lasting eight nights.

Latke is Yiddish for "pancake".

6. ...and the first bite, of course.

DID YOU KNOW?

Jews used to eat fried cheese pancakes during Hanukkah.

Once the potato was introduced to Eastern Europe in the 1800s, it replaced cheese due to its cheaper cost and reliability as a crop.

7. Licking your fingers after finishing your soufganiyot.

DID YOU KNOW?

Soufganiyah (singular) is a jelly donut topped with powdered sugar, eaten during Hanukkah.

INTERESTING FACT

Gefilte fish...

8. Is it yummy or yucky?

DID YOU KNOW?

Gefilte fish is not a real fish, it's made from a combination of other white fishes.

INTERESTING FACT

9. Holding a warm bag of fresh bagels.

DID YOU KNOW?

Bagels are traced back to the early 1600s from the Jewish communities of Poland.

INTERESTING FACT

DID YOU KNOW?

The word bagel comes from the German word "beugel", meaning "ring" (like the shape of the bagel).

QUESTION TIME!

WHICH CITY HAS THE BEST BAGELS?

Circle your answer.

TORONTO / MONTREAL / NEW YORK

10. The perfect swirl of cinnamon and chocolate in the babka.

DID YOU KNOW?

Babka originated in the Jewish communities of Poland and Ukraine in the early 1800s.

The babka got its name from a similar Polish cake - the "baba" - meaning "grandmother" in Polish.

11. The last bite of a warm, flaky boureka.

DID YOU KNOW?

Bourekas are from the Turkish word "borek" and are pastries made from thin phyllo dough stuffed with ground meat, cheese, spinach, or vegetables.

12. Opening the chocolate gelt wrapper in one peel.

DID YOU KNOW?

Gelt means money in Yiddish.

Chocolate gelt as we know it today, started in the 1920s by a company in New York.

13. Wiping the crumbs off your clothes after eating a rugelach.

DID YOU KNOW?

Rugelach is a cookie that originated in the Jewish communities of Poland. The word "rugelach" is Yiddish for "little twists".

INTERESTING FACT

14. Needing a drink of water after your mandlebroit.

DID YOU KNOW?

This cookie is like a cousin of a biscotti. From the Yiddish word "mandlbroyt" meaning "almond bread".

15. Sipping grape juice like wine.

DID YOU KNOW?
You can say the Kiddush on grape juice instead of wine.

INTERESTING FACT

16. The first crunch of matzah on Passover night.

17. All the matzah food creations like:

- Matzah Pizza
- Matzah Brei
- Matzah Bark
- Bubaleh
- Matzah Ball

DID YOU KNOW?

Each piece of matzah has about 800 holes. The holes let the air out making sure the matzah doesn't rise.

INTERESTING FACT

18. Debating which is better- sweet or savoury kugel.

DID YOU KNOW?

Kugel is an Ashkenazi Jewish dish, baked with egg noodles or potatoes.

INTERESTING FACT

19. The healing power of chicken noodle soup on a cold, winter night.

DID YOU KNOW?

Chicken soup is also known as "Jewish Penicillin".

INTERESTING FACT

20. Barely fitting the deli sandwich in your mouth because it's so big!

DID YOU KNOW?

In the early 1900s, Jewish immigrants in New York City turned their pushcart businesses into permanent stores and started selling one of the most popular fads at the time, sandwiches.

INTERESTING FACT

21. A comforting bowl of cholent for Shabbat lunch.

DID YOU KNOW?

Cholent is the original slow-cooked meal. Created in the Middle East, Ashkenazi-style cholent was first mentioned in the year 1180.

INTERESTING FACT

22. A messy mouthful of falafel. Don't forget the hummus and tahini.

DID YOU KNOW?

It is long debated who invented the falafel, but its become Israel's national dish.

INTERESTING FACT

23. The tang of a dill pickle.

DID YOU KNOW?

Jews did not invent the pickle or the pickling process, but Jewish immigrants in New York popularized the kosher dill pickle.

INTERESTING FACT

SECTION TWO
JEWISH CELEBRATIONS

24. Wishing family and friends a "Shana Tova".

DID YOU KNOW?

The Jewish calendar is always 3,760-3,761 years ahead of the of the common Gregorian calendar.

INTERESTING FACT

25. Hearing the first shofar blow on Rosh Hashana.

DID YOU KNOW?

A shofar is usually made from a ram's horn.
A ram is a male sheep.

26. Ripping the wrapper off your Hanukkah present!

27. Spelling ~~Hannukah~~ Hanukkah wrong.

DID YOU KNOW?

The tradition of giving Hannukah gifts took off in the 1950s.

The holiday can be spelled Hanukkah or Chanukah.

28. Picking which candles you want to set up on the chanukiah.

29. Savouring the beauty of the lights on the last night.

DID YOU KNOW?

A proper chanukiah needs nine candle holders. The original menorah used in the ancient Temple only had seven candle holders.

30. When you spin the dreidel perfectly on your first try.

DID YOU KNOW?

The dreidel (Yiddish for spin top) is a Jewish 'spin' on one of the oldest toys in the world- the teetotum AKA spin top.

Legend has it that Jews weren't allowed to study Torah, but they continued to do so in secret. If Greek soldiers stopped by, the kids would pull out their spin tops and pretend to be playing games.

31. Lighting the candles before Shabbat dinner.

DID YOU KNOW?

Wishing someone a "Shabbat Shalom" originated in the Sephardic communities, whereas Ashkenazi Jews more commonly said "Gut Shabbos".

INTERESTING FACT

32. Smelling the spices during Havdalah.

DID YOU KNOW?

Havdalah marks the end of Shabbat - when three stars appear in the sky.

INTERESTING FACT

33. Dressing up for Purim.

DID YOU KNOW?

Purim celebrates the survival of Persian Jewry from evil Haman.

Jews around the world dress up in costume. The first mention of this tradition was in the 1400s from an Italian Rabbi.

34. Being hit with candies after your Bar/Bat Mitzvah portion.

DID YOU KNOW?

It's a tradition to throw soft gummy candies after the kids finish their portion, it's said to help sweeten the transition to adulthood.

INTERESTING FACT

35. When the glass breaks under the Chuppah and everyone yells "Mazel Tov" at the same time.

36. Being called up for candle lighting at a Bar/Bat Mitzvah.

37. A really fun hora.

38. Being lifted up and down on a chair at a simcha.

39. Standing under a chuppah.

DID YOU KNOW?

A chuppah is a canopy with four poles that a Jewish couple stands under to get married.

INTERESTING FACT

40. The retelling of the Passover story every year.

41. Being the youngest for the Ma Nishtana.

42. Hiding (or finding) the afikoman on Passover night.

DID YOU KNOW?

The Talmud says to hide the matzah so that kids don't fall asleep during the seder!

43. A bris and baby naming celebration.

DID YOU KNOW?

A bris takes place on the 8th day of a boy's life, even if it falls on Shabbat or a holiday.

44. Sitting in a sukkah after smelling the etrog and shaking the lulav.

DID YOU KNOW?
The sukkah is meant to represent the type of shelter the Jews lived in after they were freed from slavery in Egypt.

45. Twirling the fringes of a tallit while sitting at synogauge.

DID YOU KNOW?

The fringes are called tzizit.

46. Getting a gift in a multiple of 18.

47. Saying L'chaim instead of "cheers".

DID YOU KNOW?

18 is a lucky number in Judaism. In numerology, 18 means "chai" which means "life".

SECTION THREE
CULTURAL FUN

48. Being wished a Mazel Tov!

DID YOU KNOW?

It's a yiddish phrase used to express "good fortune", used instead of saying congratulations.

"Mazel Tov" started being used in English around the 19th century.

DID YOU KNOW?

The hexagon became associated with Jews in the late 1800s when it was chosen as the symbol for the flag at the First Zionist Congress.

The Magen David is the Star of David (the David from David and Goliath).

49. Seeing a Magen David on another person.

50. Keeping Kosher... but only in the house.

51. A pinch on your cheek from bubbie.

52. Spotting a mezuzah on another house.

53. The spirit of "tikkun olam" and "tzedakah".

54. Getting to go to summer camp!

55. Playing Jewish Geogrphy and finding your connection.

56. Singing Adon Olam with a pop song tune.

57. Fun words like:

58. Saying "mazel tov" when a dish accidentally breaks.

59. Singing Hebrew songs.

60. The appreciation of humour and our comedic legends.

DID YOU KNOW?

Jews made up 3% of the American population in the late 1970s but 80% of America's comedians.

61. You don't have to be a practicing Jew to be and feel Jewish.

62. Never going hungry at a Jewish celebration.

63. Writing a note for the Western Wall.

DID YOU KNOW?

The Western Wall, is also known as the Wailing Wall or Kotel (Kotel means "wall" in Hebrew).

The Western Wall is in Jerusalem, and is the last remnant of the 2nd Temple destroyed by the Romans in 70 BCE. People write notes of prayer and leave them in the cracks of the wall.

64. Feeling at home in Israel.

DID YOU KNOW?

Israel was established as a Jewish State in 1948.

65. Reading this book... next year in Jerusalem.

66. Connecting with Jews anywhere in the world.

67. A rowdy rendition of singing "Mazel Tov and Siman Tov".

68. Everyone saying "Amen" at the same time.

69. When the song "Moshiach" comes on right after "Hava Negila" at a wedding.

70. Singing the birkat hamazon with a big group of people.

71. The idea of a bashert.

DID YOU KNOW?

Bashert is Yiddish for "destiny".

72. The strength that comes with being survivors.

Am Israel Chai

What's missing? Add your own.

73. _____
_____

74. _____
_____

75. _____
_____

76. _____
_____

77. _____
_____

www.ingramcontent.com/pod-product-compliance
Lightning Source LLC
Chambersburg PA
CBHW042029050526
44107CB00104B/817